The True Mary: Being Mrs. Browning's Poem, The Virgin Mary To The Child Jesus

Elizabeth Barrett Browning

To my dear Sister Florence
In Memory for a very
pleasant month spent together at
St. Johnland July 13th. 1878
Sister Anne

THE TRUE MARY:

BEING

MRS. BROWNING'S POEM:

"𝕿𝔥𝔢 𝖁𝔦𝔯𝔤𝔦𝔫 𝕸𝔞𝔯𝔶 𝔱𝔬 𝔱𝔥𝔢 𝕮𝔥𝔦𝔩𝔡 𝕵𝔢𝔰𝔲𝔰,"

WITH COMMENTS AND NOTES.

"*Of wedded maid and virgin mother born.*"—MILTON.

EDITED BY

W. A. MUHLENBERG.

New-York:

THOMAS WHITTAKER, No. 3 BIBLE HOUSE.
—
1868.

ST. JOHNLAND, L. I.
ORPHAN BOYS' PRESS.

INTRODUCTORY NOTE.

IT is charged by those who pay divine homage to the blessed Virgin, that they who religiously refrain from it, fail to render her any extraordinary reverence, and leave her but a common place among the saints. This may be partially true. From the tendency of one extreme to beget another, some in recoiling from anything like a deification of Mary, fear to elevate her humanity,—to guard against adoring her, they almost discourage honoring her, as the highly favored of the Lord. But this is not common. There are few Protestants who do not cherish the deepest feeling of pious veneration for the mother of our Lord. Though not hailing her regnant in Heaven, they esteem her a queenly saint, yet originally partaking of their sinful mortality. An exemplification of the true Protestant feeling on this point, we have in the poem on the following pages. None but a Protestant could have written it ; and who, whether Protestant or Catholic, we venture to ask, has ever written more worthily of Mary, with profounder or more delicate and lovely thoughts of her as the mother of the Holy Child ? No notions of an immaculate conception invest her with such genuine purity and grace, as this exquisite effort of the imagination, rich in fancy, yet sound in theology and entirely warranted by Holy Writ. For a Madonna, give us Mrs. Browning's before a Raphael's or a Correggio's, for hers is the portraiture of Mary's soul, such as in material lineaments no art could express.

The TRUE MARY is the happy designation of the ideal Mary of the poem, by the author of the notes and comments upon it, in which she is further led to consider the relation of the mother of Jesus to those who are called His brethren and sisters, and adopts the opinion sustained by high authority, that it was actually a maternal relation. The contrary is the faith of by far the greater part of Christendom, bound by ecclesiastical decrees and traditions —strange it should be entertained by any who read the evangelists in their obvious and natural meaning. The Mary of the Convent, disappears in the light of honest biblical interpretation.

But of what consequence is it, how the question be decided? Of great consequence, since the false side of it underlies the whole superstructure of Mariolatry. Take away the dogma, *Semper virgo Maria*, and the half of the papal system falls to the ground.

The superior sanctity of single life is the creed of religious Sisterhoods in the Roman communion of course, and it may be also of some such communities as are more ecclesiastical than evangelical, among Protestants. Certainly there is one of which it is not the creed,—the TRUE MARY coming from the pen of the principal of the Sisters in charge of St. Luke's Hospital.

                                                    W. A. M.

St. Johnland, L. I., October, 1867.

PREFACE.

THE following, while among the shortest of Mrs. Browning's poems, is, in many respects, one of the most perfect, and strikingly character- istic. The skill with which the transcendent dignity of the subject is maintained throughout, yet interpenetrated all along with the deepest yearnings of the mother's heart is all her own. We do not think any other pen could achieve the same.

But beyond the artistic merits of this piece, or more properly the per- fection of them, is its crystalline embodiment of Christian truth. This high Christmas Ode, this Divine Lullaby of the Virgin Mother to the Word made Flesh is both a magnificent enunciation of the doctrine of the Incarnation, and a forcible repudiating of the false worship of her whose true title is "blessedest of women."

In these days when the prime articles of our holy faith are so often found overlaid if not quite obscured by the glitter of sickly sentiment or puerile æsthetic fancies, it is something to light upon a pure gem of heavenly truth in a right royal setting—the jewel itself intact, clear, and luminous; its glory heightened and held to view, not covered by the gol- den rim which holds it. And a gem of this sort we esteem the poem be- fore us, though hitherto slightly noticed among the varied productions of its author.

It is in the hope of securing for this evangelic song—this sermon in a poem or poem of many sermons, the wider acquaintance which it deserves, that the present volume is put forth. In the further hope, also, that, from the nature of the subject, many may find in its pages something more than the amusement of a vacant hour.

A few words explanatory of the liberty taken in attempting to elucidate the more difficult passages of the poem by the comments of the appendix will be in place here. Those well versed in Mrs. Browning's style will not feel the need of any assistance of the kind. Such can refresh themselves anew with her rich and beautiful strains, and pass over unheeded all that is not hers. But to many others some help of this sort will not be superfluous. Notwithstanding the poet's great command of language and metre, she is wont, now and then, to entangle the sense of a passage by an eccentric phrase or an obscure allusion, and occasionally also her meaning is clouded by a too remote or too condensed thought, or a too involved expression of it. These are blurs upon her thrilling pages which some who would fain see all that lies beneath them, are yet without the patience to remove for themselves; and to anticipate and as far as may be, clear away any such hindrance to the full enjoyment of the present poem, is one object in offering these comments. They can be taken for what they are worth.

Another purpose, however, has been the enforcement of the leading thought of the poem, by amplifications and illustrations of the more prominent passages; a not altogether idle task, it is hoped, and interesting, if in no other way, as showing, correlatively, the degree to which Mrs. Browning's own mind was imbued with the written Word. It was alike the spring of her highest conceptions, and the silver thread running through all that tapestry of human life which her hand knew so well to weave. What else but her repleteness with Scripture is it which has kept her pen so loyal to the poet's most sacred trust—that makes her ever, in her own words,

> "Hold in high poetic duty
> Truest Truth, the fairest beauty!"

We see this especially in the subject before us, where, familiar as she was with the majesty and grace with which, as Heaven's Lady and Queen, the highest art has invested the lowly Virgin, she utters not the faintest whisper of that fond adoration into which so many half-unconsciously would have fallen.

No! Mary's authentic title and her true honor stand out erect and firm as truth itself. She is the mother of our Lord, and so in all generations counted blessed. But no more than blessed.

And this we think is the crowning pearl of the poem.

A. A.

THE VIRGIN MARY TO THE CHILD JESUS.

"But see the Virgin blest
Hath laid her Babe to rest."—*Milton's Hymn on the Nativity.*

I.

Sleep, sleep, mine Holy One!
My flesh, my Lord!—what name? I do not know
A name that seemeth not too high or low,[1]
    Too far from me or Heaven.
My Jesus, *that* is blest! that word being given
By the majestic angel whose command
Was softly as a man's beseeching said,[2]
When I and all the earth appeared to stand
    In the great overflow
Of light celestial from his wings and head.[3]
    Sleep, sleep, my saving One!

II.

And art Thou come for saving, baby-browed
And speechless Being—art Thou come for saving?
The palm that grows beside our door is bowed

By treadings of the low wind from the south,[4]
A restless shadow through the chamber waving :
Upon its bough a bird sings in the sun ;
But Thou, with that close slumber on Thy mouth
Dost seem of wind and sun already weary.
Art come for saving, O my weary One ?

III.

Perchance this sleep that shutteth out the dreary
Earth-sounds and motions, opens on Thy soul
    High dreams on fire with God ;[5]
High songs that make the pathways where they roll
More bright than stars do theirs ;[6] and visions new
Of Thine eternal Nature's old abode.[7]
    Suffer this mother's kiss,
    Best thing that earthly is,
To glide the music and the glory through,
Nor narrow in Thy dream the broad upliftings
    Of any seraph wing ![8]
Thus, noiseless thus. Sleep, sleep, my dreaming One!

IV.

The slumber of His lips meseems to run
Through *my* lips to mine heart ; to all its shiftings
Of sensual life, bringing contrariousness
In a great calm.[9] I feel I could lie down

As Moses did, and die,* — and then live most.
I am 'ware of you, heavenly Presences,
That stand with your peculiar light unlost—
Each forehead with a high thought for a crown
Unsunn'd i' the sunshine![10] I am 'ware. Ye throw
No shade against the wall! How motionless
Ye round me with your living statuary,
While through your whiteness, in and outwardly
Continual thoughts of God appear to go,
Like Light's soul in itself![11] I bear, I bear
To look upon the dropt lids of your eyes,
Though their external shining testifies
To that beatitude within which were
Enough to blast an eagle at his sun.
I fall not on my sad clay face before ye —
  I look on His; I know
My spirit which dilateth with the woe
   Of His mortality,
   May well contain your glory.[12]
   Yea, drop your lids more low, —
Ye are but fellow-worshippers with me!
   Sleep, sleep, my worshipped One!

V.

We sate among the stalls at Bethlehem.
The dumb kine from their fodder turning them,

---

* It is a Jewish tradition that Moses died of the kisses of God's lips.

Softened their horned faces
To almost human gazes[13]
Toward the newly Born.
The simple shepherds from the star-lit brooks
Brought visionary looks,[14]
As yet in their astonied hearing rung
The strange, sweet angel-tongue.
The magi of the East, in sandals worn,
Knelt reverent, sweeping round,
With long pale beards, their gifts upon the ground,—
The incense, myrrh, and gold
These baby hands were impotent to hold.
So, let all earthlies and celestials wait
Upon Thy royal state!
Sleep, sleep, my kingly One!

VI.

I am not proud — meek angels, ye invest
New meeknesses to hear such utterance rest
On mortal lips, — 'I am not proud'[15] — *not proud!*
Albeit in my flesh God sent His Son,
Albeit over Him my head is bowed,
As others bow before Him, still mine heart
Bows lower than their knees. O centuries
That roll, in vision, your futurities
My future grave athwart, —
Whose murmurs seem to reach me while I keep

Watch o'er this sleep, —
Say of me as the Heavenly said — 'Thou art
The blessedest of women !' — blessedest,
Not holiest, not noblest — no high name,
Whose height misplaced may pierce me like a shame,
When I sit meek in heaven ![16]

VII.

For me — for me —
God knows that I am feeble like the rest ![17]
I often wandered forth, more child than maiden,
Among the midnight hills of Galilee, ·

Whose summits looked heaven-laden,
Listening to silence, as it seemed to be
God's voice, so soft yet strong — so fain to press
Upon my heart as Heaven did on the height,
And waken up its shadows by a light,
And show its vileness by a holiness.[18]
Then I knelt down most silent like the night,

Too self-renounced for fears,[19]
Raising my small face to the boundless blue
Whose stars did mix and tremble in my tears.
God heard *them* falling after — with His dew.[20]

VIII.

So, seeing my corruption, can I see
This Incorruptible now born of me —[21]
This fair new Innocence no sun did chance

To shine on, (for even Adam was no child)[22]
Created from my nature all defiled, —
This mystery, from out mine ignorance, —
Nor feel the blindness, stain, corruption, more
Than others do, or *I* did heretofore? —
Can hands wherein such burden pure has been,
Not open with the cry 'unclean, unclean!'
More oft than any else beneath the skies?
  Ah King, ah Christ, ah Son!.
The kine, the shepherds, the abased wise,
  Did all less lowly wait
  Than I, upon Thy state! —
  Sleep, sleep, my kingly One!

    IX.

Art Thou a King, then? Come, His universe,
  Come, crown me Him a King!
Pluck rays from all such stars as never fling
  Their light where fell a curse,
And make a crowning for this kingly brow!
What is my word?[23] — Each empyreal star
  Sits in a sphere afar
  In shining ambuscade.
  The child-brow, crowned by none,
  Keeps its unchildlike shade.
  Sleep, sleep, my crownless One!

X.

Unchildlike shade! No other babe doth wear
An aspect very sorrowful, as Thou. —[24]
No small babe-smiles, my watching heart has seen,
To float like speech the speechless lips between;
No dovelike cooing in the golden air,
No quick short joys of leaping babyhood.

　　Alas, our earthly good
In heaven thought evil, seems too good for Thee:[25]

　　Yet sleep, my weary One!

XI.

And then the drear sharp tongue of prophecy,
With the dread sense of things which shall be done,
Doth smite me inly, like a sword — a sword? —
(*That* 'smites the Shepherd,')[26] then I think aloud
The words 'despised,' — 'rejected,' — every word
Recoiling into darkness as I view

　　The DARLING on my knee.
Bright angels, — move not! — lest ye stir the cloud
Betwixt my soul and His futurity![27]
I must not die, with mother's work to do,

　　And could not live — and see.

XII.

　　It is enough to bear
　　This image still and fair —
　　This holier in sleep,

Than a saint at prayer:
This aspect of a Child
Who never sinned or smiled —
This Presence in an infant's face:
This sadness most like love,
This love than love more deep,
This weakness like Omnipotence
It is so strong to move!
Awful is this watching place,
Awful what I see from hence —
A King, without regalia,
A God, without the thunder,
A child without the heart for play:
Ay, a Creator rent asunder
From his first glory and cast away
On his own world, for me alone
To hold in hands created, crying — Son!

XIII.

That tear fell not on *Thee!*
Beloved, yet Thou stirrest in Thy slumber,
Thou, stirring not for glad sounds out of number
Which through the vibratory palm-trees run
    From summer wind and bird,
    So quickly hast Thou heard
    A tear fall silently? —[28]
Wak'st Thou, O loving One?

COMMENTS AND NOTES.

COMMENTS AND NOTES.

1.

My flesh, my Lord! what name? I do not know
A name that seemeth not too high or low.

How shall Mary address Him who is at once her offspring
and her Lord? Any fond earthly name akin to her own
would be unworthy the eternal Son of God, and a name all
divine would separate Him too far from His human mother.

2.

Whose command
Was softly as a man's beseeching said.

The angel's direction to Mary as to the name of the Holy
Child was as gentle and gracious in its utterance as if it had
been the kind request of a fellow-being.

3.

When I and all the earth appeared to stand
In the great overflow
Of light celestial from his wings and head.

When Mary's faith received the great announcement, that
of her was to be born He who should save His people from
their sins, it was as though the light emanating from the
angel overstreamed and irradiated herself and all mankind.

A beautiful suggestion here of the ultimate issue of the
work of redemption, when the beatified hosts of the redeemed
shall be sharers with the angels in the everlasting glory.

4.
The palm that grows beside our door is bowed
By treadings of the low wind, etc.

It is not easy to see the force of this passage. Perhaps it is meant to express a tender lament, akin to that of the tenth stanza.

5.
Perchance this sleep that shutteth out the dreary
Earth-sounds and motions, opens on Thy soul
High dreams on fire with God.

The sleep of the Holy Child, closing His senses to the sights and sounds of human sin and misery, may give to His soul transcendent dreams of celestial glory.

6.
High songs that make the pathways where they roll
More bright than stars do theirs.

The poet conceives the hymnings of cherubim and seraphim to be part of the Saviour's dream — songs of rapturous adoration which diffuse throughout the angelic host a holy joy, or spiritual brightness, exceeding that of the highest material splendor.

7.
............and visions new
Of Thine eternal Nature's old abode.

That is, new manifestations, while dreaming, of the Heaven whence He came.

8.
Nor narrow in Thy dream the broad upliftings
Of any seraph wing.

Mary, in kissing noiselessly the lips of the sleeping Child, supplicates that the one pure thing of earth—a mother's kiss, may become present to His consciousness amid the glories of His dream, yet not so far recall Him to earth as to cause the slightest interruption of that dream, not so much as the folding of a seraph's wing.

9.
..........bringing contrariousness
In a great calm.

Bringing the *opposite* of all the tumultuous emotions of the heart, viz.: an inexpressible calmness—the marvellously tranquillizing effect of the contact of Mary's lips with those of the Holy Child.

10.
I am 'ware of you, heavenly Presences,
That stand with your peculiar light unlost,—
Each forehead with a high thought for a crown,
Unsunn'd i' th' sunshine.

Mary becomes aware of the presence of the ministering angels, each one with his original holiness unimpaired. A contrast is implied with the fallen angels "from eternal splendors flung, their glory vanished."

"*Each forehead with a high thought for a crown*" is a noble conception. Milton's angels "bind their resplendent locks" with flowers of amaranth inwoven with gold, gorgeously and beautifully symbolizing their immortality, no doubt, but we think Mrs. Browning's the more exalted crowning. Indeed, her creations of this kind, throughout, are remarkably independent of those elements of sensuous, physical beauty which make so largely the material of all the angels given to our view out of the Scriptures.

11.
While through your whiteness, in and outwardly,
Continual thoughts of God appear to go,
Like Light's soul in itself!

The idea conveyed in this fine simile may perhaps be rendered thus: The corporeity of the angels is an embodiment of light, and their impulses and emotions are as the soul or

essence of this light; vibrating inwardly in adoring love to
God, and outwardly in services of God's good-will to man.

> 12.
> I fall not on my sad clay face before ye,—
> I look on His; I know
> My spirit which dilateth with the woe
> Of His mortality,
> May well contain your glory.

The great angels standing round her "in bright harnessed
order serviceable," do not overpower this mortal woman, child
of dust as she is. She does not fall down upon her face
before them; she looks upon the countenance of the Child
Jesus, and her soul, occupied with the sorrows of His humanity, can bear unmoved the created glory of His angelic
attendants—fellow-worshippers with herself.

> 13.
> Softened their horned faces
> To almost human gazes.

That is, gazed with almost human looks upon the newly-
born Saviour. Mary's thoughts revert to the night of the
Nativity and its attendant circumstances, in connection with
the homage which she claims for Him from the angels and
from all others, whether "earthlies" or "celestials."

> 14.
> The simple shepherds from the star-lit brooks
> Brought visionary looks.

When the shepherds came to Bethlehem in search of the
Babe whose birth the angels had made known to them, their
countenances still expressed the awe and amazement inspired
by the heavenly vision.

> 15.
> I am not proud—meek angels, ye invest
> New meeknesses to hear such utterance rest
> On mortal lips.

"*Ye invest new meeknesses,*" that is, invest or clothe yourselves anew with meekness, or grow meeker still. The thought seems to be that if she in whose flesh God sent His Son can affirm that she is not proud, no other, even the highest created being, can have room to glory. But humility is a delicate and sensitive grace, "gone if it but look upon itself;" it could only be a most rare and singular endowment of it that would allow its possessor thus to declare 'I am not proud'; perhaps so much could not be assumed for any other than the blessed Mother of our Lord, for in none other could those circumstances come together which both produced and proved this rare humility. A subsequent passage in the poem illustrates and explains this.

16.
O centuries
That roll, in vision, your futurities
My future grave athwart,—
Whose murmurs seem to reach me while I keep
Watch o'er this sleep,—
Say of me as the Heavenly said—"Thou art
The blessedest of women!"—blessedest,
Not holiest, not noblest—no high name,
Whose height misplaced may pierce me like a shame,
When I sit meek in heaven!

This apostrophe of the blessed Virgin's is highly significant. Sitting in the silent chamber, the Holy Child still asleep upon her lap, presentiments of the future rise before her. She hears, in the murmurs of the ages yet to come, as they roll with their traditions over her grave, the various epithets by which men have arrogated to her the attributes of the Supreme. Her holy and humble heart is roused to pathetic deprecation of the wrong thus done to herself, and she charges the generations as they pass to speak of her only as "the Heavenly"—the angel—did, as "Blessedest of women," not call her by misplaced high titles which, reaching her knowledge in heaven, in her place among the meek in heart, would pierce her with shame.

Beautiful this, and entirely consistent with the lowliness of the Lord's handmaiden as expressed in her own inspired song at the visitation of Elizabeth. For what is the burden of that first Christian Hymn? Not exultation in her coming glorification into a demi-goddess — not that she is going to be the mother of Deity—a mediatrix controlling the mind of the one Mediator — a Lady Regnant in the churches — a Queen in Heaven hearing prayers and dispensing favors to the faithful below—no! but "My soul doth magnify the Lord, and my spirit rejoiceth in God my Saviour." Mary's spirit is filled with holy joy at the near advent of her Saviour and ours, and she magnifies with meek gladness the great goodness of the Lord, who passing by the rich and noble of her tribe, has chosen her, one of the humblest of the house of David, through whom to fulfil this first and greatest of the promises; thus making her, throughout all generations, the most blessed of women.

It is worth while from the importance of the subject to pause here a moment and consider, as closely as we may, wherein this pre-eminent blessedness of Mary's consisted. Was it solely in her high privilege of being the mother of our Lord? Or was it not, at least correspondingly, in that pre-eminent endowment of faith, obedience, and the other heavenly virtues which must have accompanied her election to this high privilege?

On a certain occasion in our Saviour's public ministry when a woman of the crowd, moved by His wonderful words, cried out, "Blessed is the mother that bare thee"! the Lord immediately replied, "Yea, rather blessed are they that hear the word of God and keep it." He did not deny that Mary was indeed blessed in being His mother, but emphatically declared that there is a higher blessedness than this union with Him in the ties of earth, viz.: that of those who believing and obeying the word of God are joined to Him, the perfectly obedient Son of the Father, in a spiritual and everlasting relationship.

And was not the Virgin Mary's an exalted degree of this

blessedness also? We may not doubt it. No reverent Christian mind can think of the mother of our Lord but as combining in her character all that is tender and excellent in woman with all that is richest in God's gifts of grace. Nor are we left to our imagination on this point. The sacred story while remarkably reticent as to Mary's circumstances and feelings *after* the birth of the Holy Child, mentioning her very seldom, and then, for the most part incidentally, gives us a beautiful insight both of her outward and her inward life *before* the transcendent event transpires.* And if, on the one hand, we are sufficiently free from those false ideas of the blessed Virgin which blind us to a just conception of her as a woman, and on the other hand, are not unduly held back by a fear of too much reverence, from contemplating the holiness by which she must have been distinguished, we shall find in those early pages of the gospel, so gloriously illumined by the Holy Spirit, the outlines of a faith and obedience which made Mary, we are ready to say, the very first of those who are supremely blest because they "hear the word of God and keep it."

Look, as illustrative of this, at the extraordinary test to which Mary's faith was put in accepting the communication of the angel. She was an espoused, that is, a betrothed maiden, was poor, unprotected. The verification of the angelic announcement might cost her, as indeed for a while it seemed imminent it would cost her, the loss of her promised husband, her home, her character, and exposure to public disgrace. Was it not then a perfect faith, a most true obedience, and self-renouncing humility which, confronting such possibilities, demurred not at them but answered, with meek and ready obedience, afterwards rewarded by an inspiration of holy joy,

---

* The veil is lifted about her in all that concerns her motherhood,—in all that through her brings out the true humanity of His nature ; the veil is dropped when this office is closed, and the *Magnificat* sung, and Christ, the Son of Man, is shown as such by her, His mother, to men."—[DR. WHARTON'S *Silence of the Scriptures.*

"Behold the handmaid of the Lord, be it unto me according
to Thy word." Shall we err in affirming that the blessedness
of Mary's surpassing motherhood was perfected by the
greater blessedness of surpassing faith and obedience?

17.

For me—

For me—I'm feeble like the rest!—

That is, a woman of like infirmities with other women, thus
disclaiming aught in her nature essentially different from the
rest of the race; certainly then, the figment of her immaculate
conception, which, if true, would reduce the stupendous
central fact of the Incarnation to the sequence of a prior
miracle. The concrete thought underlying this and the suc-
ceeding stanza of the poem seems to be that Mary was not
raised by her high dignity to a condition so far above our
proper humanity as to do away in her with the elements of
our fallen nature. And this is in harmony with the glimpses
which the Scriptures give us of the mother of our Lord, of
whom it is difficult to trace any lineament in the legendary
portraits of the "Immaculate Mother of God." Mary's deification destroys her identity. Singularly few, however, it may
be remarked here, are these glimpses of Mary in the authentic
record.* She appears there only four or five times after the
infancy of our Lord, and as though to guard believers from
the very errors into which so large a portion of Christendom has fallen, these appearances with one exception, (that
at the Cross), are invariably accompanied by an almost rebuke
from our Lord of her motherly interference; or if this be too
strong, certainly with a distinct intimation that in fulfilling
the end to which He was born, their relation as son and
mother has no longer a place. A signal instance of this
occurs in connection with the healing of the withered hand.
Mary had probably heard that the Pharisees were holding a

* See Note B.

council to destroy Jesus, and goes with her sons to rescue Him from the danger. She cannot reach Him for the crowd. Some one conveys a message for her : "Thy mother and Thy brethren are without, desiring to speak with Thee." Our Lord replies to him that told Him, "Who is my mother, and who are my brethren ; for whosoever shall do the will of my Father which is in Heaven, the same is my brother, and sister, and mother."

Again, while we gather from a few such passages in the gospels that Mary watched with the solicitude of the holiest mother's love the footsteps of her Son, (the mystery of whose being she pondered but could not penetrate,) without receiving any of those endearing returns which common mothers enjoy ; we also gather from the same source, that her daily life was in other respects much that of any other Jewish matron. She was the carpenter's wife and the mother of his children, James, Joses, and the rest ;* her marriage with Joseph differing only from other godly marriages in the marvellous events connected with the betrothed before its consummation. Taking the words of the sacred narrative in their obvious and natural sense, all this, we think is plain ; unless, indeed, we range ourselves with those who, assuming for the blessed mother of our Lord a grace of their own devising, disparage the marriage relation, and make an anomaly of that wedded home which was divinely honored as the protection of the infancy and childhood of the Incarnate Son of God.

But there are others who without surrendering themselves to that system of pious romance, or sentimental devotion, to call it by no graver name, yet deny to Mary any other than her one miraculous motherhood, and so make Joseph's marriage with the blessed Virgin barren of that "heritage and gift of the Lord" which, in the estimation of a Jew, was indispensable to all heaven-blest wedlock. But Joseph, the

---

* See Note A.

support of Mary in her utmost need, and the foster-father of
our Lord Jesus Christ, an unblest, childless man, is not con-
gruous to our Christian common sense.

A question suggests itself, in this connection, with regard
to the tarrying behind of the Child Jesus at Jerusalem without the knowledge of Joseph and Mary. If Jesus was the
sole claimant of Mary's maternal love, was it not most extraordinary and inexplicable that she could for a moment think
of setting out from the crowded city without her precious boy
by her side, at least without ascertaining where, and with
whom He was? Would any tender mother of our acquaintance have done so by an only darling? But it is easier to
understand this if we may suppose that Mary's homeward
bound steps were quickened by motherly anxiety for other
and younger children left behind at Nazareth. We can
imagine that thoughts of these might, for the time, so engross
her as to exclude solicitude about her first-born Son, whose
proved dutifulness besides may have given her an habitual
freedom from anxiety on His account. And in Mary's half-
chiding words when at length she finds the Child Jesus in the
Temple, is there not a corresponding suggestion? "Son, why
hast thou thus dealt with us? Thy father and I have sought
thee, sorrowing." She associates Joseph with herself in
wonted household phrase as her husband and the father of
her children, one among whom, in His humiliation, "the Only
Begotten of the Father," deigns to be considered. "Is not
this the carpenter's son? Is not his mother called Mary?
and his brethren James, and Joses, and Simon, and Judas?"*

Yet again. The deep suggestions of the poem, bringing
before us the mother of our Lord complete in all the qualities
and functions of a true and sanctified womanhood, do Mary
far more real honor than all the æsthetic fictions of her wor-
shippers. She is not an abstraction or mystical being, not a
sinless, half-celestial creature, but a flesh and blood woman,

* Matt. xiii : 55.

distinguished indeed above other women in her exalted
mother joys and her piercing mother sorrows, yet bearing the
one and the other of these in the strength of God's grace, like
other believing mothers in their lower maternity.   She is not
above our sympathy, neither is she below our truest love and
reverence as a woman of all women the most "highly favored
of the Lord," and the foremost of those "who hear the word
of God and keep it."

> "Thou shalt be crowned, but not alone ;
> No lonely pomp shall weigh thee down ;
> Crown'd with the myriads round His throne,
> And casting at His feet Thy crown."

18.

And waken up its shadows b ay light,
And show its vileness by a holiness.

As the dark shadows of the hills were brought out and in-
tensified by their contrast with the starlit sky, so was Mary
made more vividly conscious of the sinfulness of her nature
by the sense of God's holiness pressing upon her soul in the
midnight silence of those solitudes.

19.

Too self-renounced for fears.

Entire forgetfulness of self begets immunity from fear on
one's own account.   Or, understanding the words more
spiritually, a heart taken up with God, that is, wholly pos-
sessed with a sense of God's goodness and its own unworthi-
ness, has that "perfect love which casteth out fear."

20.

....heard *them* falling after—with his dew.

Heard her tears fall with the dew.

21.

So, seeing my corruption, can I see
This Incorruptible now born of me—

Mary proceeds to show upon what grounds she can affirm

she is not proud; that, understanding her own depravity of
nature, she could not behold this All-holy One born of her
and not feel the sinfulness of sin more than others do, or than
she did formerly.

22.

This fair new Innocence no sun did chance
To shine on, (for even Adam was no child).

Adam was created a fully developed man, Cain was not
born until after the fall, therefore the sun had never shone
upon an essentially sinless babe until our Lord came into the
world. The Child Jesus was the one only true "Holy Innocent."

23.

What is my word?

That is, "what power have I to command the universe"?
With passionate eagerness for the rights of her Son and King
Mary has called upon Creation to come and crown Him—has
bidden the stars undarkened by sin yield their rays to make
His regalia. Then recollects herself, "What is my word," etc.

Doubtless the poet had more in her mind in this passage
than simply a rhetorical figure. It is in harmony with the
key-note of the poem here again to understand a rebuke of
that wrong estimate of the mother of our Lord which in our
day has developed into the assumption for her of some of the
essential attributes of Deity.

The vindicators of the worship of the Virgin argue that its
effect is to heighten the glory of our Lord Jesus Christ
by protecting the doctrine of the Incarnation, and find some
show of truth for this in the first use of the term Mother of
God.* But how many of the thousands who invoke the Virgin Mary are intellectually capable of the nice and subtle dis-
tinctions as to kinds and degrees of worship involved in such a

See Note C.

theory. Nothing is possible to the majority of these, but to take all such devotions and whatever in æsthetics is employed to illustrate them in their gross and palpable meaning.

Several years ago in one of the art-lined rooms of the Pitti Palace, Florence, there was a large picture which as often as the door was opened to strangers, had always its especial group of admirers. The painting, said to be a Guido, was in itself a masterpiece, but its chief attraction was the religious sentiment it expressed, which was very tenderly and beautifully brought out. The subject was the Pardoned Magdalene. The principal figures, life-size, were the Virgin and Child, the recording Angel, and the Magdalene kneeling. The Angel supported a large open folio, the Book of Doom, in front of the Virgin, who, guiding the finger of the infant Saviour, was erasing with it the sins there written against the penitent. Now what is the teaching of that picture? Whom does it depict as the true Absolver of the Magdalene—the Supreme Arbiter of forgiveness to her? Certainly not the Lord Jesus Christ. It would need but few words with any of the simple Florentines, standing so admiringly before it, to be convinced that its effect upon them was altogether to magnify the clemency of "Our Lady." To them she beamed forth afresh from the living canvas as "Queen of Mercy," "Protectress from the Divine Justice," "Singular Refuge of the Lost," or some other of that multitude of titles and attributes which characterize the cultus of the Virgin in its fullest development!*

24.

Unchildlike shade!—no other babe doth wear
An aspect very sorrowful, as Thou.

Whether the infancy of our blessed Lord was indeed marked by such forecastings of the passion of the "Man of Sorrows" we cannot know. In the single verse in the gospel

* See Liguori's "Glories of Mary." Translated and published, London, 1852.

C

of St. Luke, which is all that is given us of the Saviour's earliest years, we read : "The child grew and waxed strong in spirit, filled with wisdom, and the grace of God was upon him." Whatever be the exact meaning of the words "filled with wisdom," an infancy, in any sense, so endowed must have had an "unchildlike" gravity.

25.
Alas, our earthly good
In heaven thought evil, seems too good for Thee.

We do not believe that the "earthly good"—the joyous babyhood here so charmingly pictured—is deemed "evil" in heaven. The morbid sadness which sometimes tinges Mrs. Browning's verse may have given rise to this thought. Nevertheless, it is an allowable and an affecting conjecture that our Divine Redeemer, in assuming the full burden of our fallen nature, may have foregone, even in infancy, every innocent earthly delight.

26.
Doth smite me inly like a sword—a sword?
That smites the Shepherd.

"A sword shall pierce through thine own soul, also," St. Simeon had declared to the Blessed Virgin at the presentation of Jesus in the Temple.* Mary is represented as recalling these words and thence passing on to the thought of that older prophecy of a yet heavier sword in the Book of Zechariah.†

27.
Bright angels,—move not!—lest ye stir the cloud
Betwixt my soul and His futurity!

With the ministering angels within sight Mary may be able to withdraw her thoughts from "the dread sense of things which shall be done," *i. e.*, the angels are themselves

* See Note D.　　　　† Zech. xiii : 7.

the cloud hiding the dark future from her gaze. This re-
minds one of Raphael's Madonna di Foligni, where what
appear, at, first sight, as delicate masses of silvery clouds
filling the azure heavens, prove upon closer inspection to be
"billowy hosts" of angels.

28.

So quickly hast Thou heard
A tear fall silently?—
Wak'st Thou, O loving One?—

This is exquisite. The Holy Child, unmoved in his
slumbers by the singing of the birds and other happy sounds,
wakes instantly at the falling of a tear—a lovely suggestion of
the infinite pity and perfect sympathy of our Lord Jesus
Christ.

NOTE A.

In arguing at all against their (James, Joses, etc.,) being the real brethren of Jesus, far too much stress has been laid on the assumed indefiniteness of meaning attached to the word "brother" in Scripture. In all the adduced cases it will be seen that when the word is used in any but its proper sense, the context prevents the possibility of confusion; and indeed in the only two exceptional instances (not metaphorical), viz.: those in which Lot and Jacob are respectively called "brothers" of Abraham and Laban, the word is only extended so far as to mean "nephew"; and it must be remembered that even these exceptions are quoted from a single book, seventeen centuries earlier than the gospels. If then the word "brethren," as repeatedly applied to James, etc., really mean "cousins" or "kinsmen," it will be the *only* instance of such an application in which no data are given to correct the laxity of meaning. Again, no really parallel case can be quoted from the New Testament, except in merely rhetorical and tropical passages; whereas when "nephews" are meant they are always specified as such, as in Col. iv. 10, Acts xxiii. 16. There is therefore no adequate warrant in the language alone, to take "brethren" as meaning "relatives"; and therefore the *a priori* presumption is in favor of a literal acceptation of the term. We have dwelt the more strongly on this point, because it seems to have been far too easily assumed that no importance is to be attached to the mere fact of their being *invariably* called Christ's brethren; whereas this consideration alone goes far to prove that they really were so.

There are, however, three traditions respecting them. They are first mentioned (Matt. xiii. 55,) in a manner which would certainly lead an unbiassed mind to conclude that they were our Lord's uterine brothers. "Is not this the carpenter's son? is not *his mother* called Mary? *and his brethren* James, and Joses, and Judas, and Simon? *and his sisters*, are they not all with us?" But since we find that there was a "Mary, the mother of James and Joses" (Matt. xxvii : 56), and that a "James and Judas (?)" were sons of Alphæus (Luke vi : 15, 16,) the most general tradition is :

I. That they were all our Lord's first cousins, the sons of Alphæus, (or Clopas—not Cleopas. Alford G'k. Test., Matt. x. 3,) and Mary the sister of the Virgin. This tradition is accepted by Papias, Jerome (Cat. Script. Ecc. 2), Augustine, and the Latin Church generally, and is now the one most commonly received. Yet there seem to be overwhelming arguments against it : for (1) The reasoning entirely depends on three very doubtful assumptions, viz.: (a.) That "his mother's sister" (John xix : 25,) must be in apposition with "Mary the wife of Cleopas," which would be improbable, if only on the ground that it supposes two sisters to have had the same name—a supposition substantiated by no parallel cases. [Wieseler (Comp. Mark. 15 : 40,) thinks that Salome, the wife of Zebedee, is intended by "his mother's sister."] (b.) That "Mary the mother of James" was the wife of Alphæus. (c.) That Cleopas, or more correctly Clopas, whose wife Mary was, is identical with Alphæus, which may be the case, although it cannot be proved. (2.) If his cousins were meant, it would be signally untrue that "neither did his brethren believe on him" (John vii : 5, sq.), for in all probability three out of the four (viz.: James the Less, Matthew (or Levi), and Jude, the brother (?) of James,) were actual Apostles. We do not see how this objection can be removed. (3) It is quite unaccountable that these ("brethren of the

Lord,") if they were only His cousins, should be always mentioned in conjunction with the Virgin Mary, and never with their own mother Mary, who was both alive and in constant attendance upon our Lord. (4) They are generally spoken of as *distinct from* the Apostles; see Acts 1:14; 1 Cor. 9:5; and Jude (17) seems to clearly imply that he himself was not an Apostle. It seems to us that these four objections are quite adequate to set aside the very slight grounds for identifying the "brethren of the Lord" with the "sons of Alphæus."

II. A second tradition accepted by Hilary, Epiphanius, and the Greek fathers generally, makes them the sons of Joseph by a former marriage with a certain Escha or Salome of the tribe of Judah; indeed Epiphanius (Hæres. 29 : 4,) even mentions the supposed order. of birth of the four sons and two daughters. But Jerome (Com. on Matt. 12 : 49), slights this as a mere conjecture, borrowed from the "Deliramenta Apocryphorum;" and Origen says that it was taken from the Gospel of St. Peter. The only shadow of ground for its possibility is the apparent difference of age between Joseph and the Virgin.

III. They are assumed to have been the offspring of a Levirate marriage between Joseph and the wife of his deceased brother Clopas. But apart from all evidence, it is obviously idle to examine so arbitrary an assumption.

The arguments *against* their being the sons of the Virgin after the birth of our Lord are founded on (1) The almost constant tradition of *aei-parthenos*. Still the tradition was not universal; it was denied, for instance, by large numbers called Antidicomarianitæ and Helvidiani. To quote Ezek. 44 : 2 as any argument on the question is plainly absurd. (2) On the fact that on the cross Christ commended his mother to the care of St. John; but this is easily explicable on the ground of his brethren's apparent disbelief in Him at that time, though they seem to have been converted very soon afterward.*

* See Note D.

(3) On the identity of their names with those of the sons of Alphæus. This argument loses all weight when we remember the constant recurrence of names in Jewish families, and the extreme commonness of these particular names. In the New Testament alone there may be at least five contemporary Jameses and several Judes, not to mention the twenty-one Simons, seventeen Joses, and sixteen Judes mentioned by Josephus.

On the other hand the arguments *for* their being our Lord's uterine brothers are numerous, and taken collectively, to an unprejudiced mind almost irresistible, although singly they are open to objections ; *e. g.* (1) The words in Luke 2 : 7, (2) Matt. 1 : 25, to which Alford justly remarks only one meaning could have been attached but for preconceived theories. (3) The general tone of the Gospels on the subject, since they are constantly spoken of with the Virgin Mary, and with no shadow of a hint that they were not her own children (Matt. 12 : 46. Mark 3 : 31, etc.) It can we think be hardly denied that any one of these arguments is singly stronger than those produced on the other side.

To sum up then, we have seen (1) That the "brethren of the Lord" could hardly have been identical with the sons of Alphæus, and (2) That we have no grounds for supposing them to have been the sons of Joseph by a previous, or (3) a Levirate marriage ; that the arguments in favor of their being actual brothers of our Lord are cogent, and that the tradition on the other side is not sufficiently weighty or unanimous to set them aside.

Finally, this tradition of the perpetual virginity of the mother of our Lord (which any one may hold, if he will, as one of the "pie credibilia," (Jer. Taylor Duct. Dub. II. 3, 6,) is easily accounted for by the general error on the inferiority of the wedded to the virgin state.—[*From* SMITH's *Bible Dictionary on "Brethren of the Lord."*

NOTE B.

In the narrative of our Lord's divine work as the Mediator between God and man, Mary is throughout carefully screened from our eye. Others who were employed by Him as missionaries of mercy and of power, are mentioned to us in this their sacred capacity; Mary never. A centurian intercedes for a sick servant, and the intercession was effective. His disciples cry unto Him, "Lord save us, we perish," and He arose and calmed the sea. A certain ruler worshipped Him saying, "My daughter is even now dead, but come and lay Thy hand upon her and she shall live; and He came and took her by the hand, and the maid arose." In many instances after our Lord's ascension, the apostles applied to Him for miraculous power, and in each case the prayer was granted. But we hear of no intercession made to Him by Mary except that in Cana of Galilee, and in that case the intercession was rebuked.

So also, we have frequent mention of specific delegations of power. Thus, at one time, the Lord "called His twelve disciples together, and gave them power and authority over all devils, and to cure diseases." Then again, He sent out seventy with other powers. Then, after the resurrection, the eleven were charged with the great work of evangelizing the world, and for this were endowed with miraculous gifts. And in the infant Church, as narrated in the Acts of the Apostles, particular apostles were specifically employed in miraculous work. Yet in no case is Mary mentioned as thus delegated or thus empowered.

And so, again, we are pointed to those who were the intimate attendants, and as it were, counsellors of the Lord during His obedience and passion. There were Peter, and James, and John, who were with Him at Tabor and Gethsemane. There was John whom He so peculiarly loved, and who leaned on the Lord's bosom at the Paschal Supper. There was Peter to whom He said, "Blessed art thou, Simon Barjona. Thou art Peter; on this rock"—on the confession of my divinity—"I will build my Church." Peter, to whom He gave the keys; Peter, on whom He looked with such melting tenderness in the judgment hall; Peter, to whom He gave the final command, "Feed my sheep." There were Mary Magdalene, and Joanna, and Mary the mother of James, who are specified as first at the sepulchre. There were the disciples with whom He communed at Emmaus, and those whom He made the chosen witnesses of His ascension. Yet there is no notice of Mary in either of these relations, or as in any way the partaker of the counsels of the Lord when in His divine work. She was, it is true, at the cross; but we are informed of this only incidentally from the fact that she was committed to John's care, not John to her, as would have been the case had she been assigned a position of anything like power; and it is the *home* of John, not his office, with which her name is to be allied. She is not mentioned as having even seen the Lord after the resurrection; she performs no act in the New Testament Church. That she associated with the disciples at Jerusalem after His ascension we are indeed informed, but beyond this, there is no record. Of her subsequent life and death, copious as is the sacred narrative in other respects, not a word is told."—[DR. WHARTON'S *Silence of the Scriptures.*

NOTE C.

Down to the time of the Nestorian controversy the *cultus* of the Blessed Virgin would appear to have been wholly external to the Church, and to have been regarded as heretical. But the Nestorian controversies produced a great change of sentiment in men's minds. Nestorius had maintained, or at least it was the tendency of Nestorianism to maintain, not only that our Lord had two natures, the divine and the human (which was right), but also that He was two persons, in such sort that the child born of Mary was not divine, but merely an ordinary human being, until the divinity subsequently united itself to Him. This was condemned by the Council of Ephesus in the year 431, and the title THEOTOKOS, loosely translated "Mother of God," was sanctioned. The object of the Council and of the Anti-Nestorians was in no sense to add honor to the mother, but to maintain the true doctrine with respect to the Son. For now the title Theotokos became a shibboleth ; and in art the representation of the Madonna and Child became the expression of orthodox belief. Very soon the purpose for which the title and the picture were first sanctioned became forgotten, and the veneration of St. Mary began to spread within the Church as it had previously existed external to it. The legends, too, were no longer treated so roughly as before. The Gnostics were not now objects of dread. Nestorians and afterwards Iconoclasts were objects of hatred. The old fables were winked at, and thus they "became the mythology of Christianity universally credited among the southern nations of Europe, while many of the dogmas which they are grounded upon, have, as a natural consequence, crept into the faith."—[LORD LINDSAY, *Christian Art.*

NOTE D.

" There stood by the cross of Jesus Mary his mother," John
19 : 25. *Mater Dolorosa* is Mary indeed under the cross, as
Simeon had predicted ; yet she stood, with all her grief, in
the strength of faith and love ; she *could* thus stand near the
cross, not far from the crucifying soldiers! She held her
spirit under command, as alone became her dignity and her
experience. That which first the Fathers and then the series
of Catholic writers describe or invent of the anguish and de-
spair of the Saviour's mother under the cross has been amply
protested against.   *   *   *

" Woman, behold thy son," John 19 : 21. But why does He
not call her mother?   *   *   The chief reason is this, that her
relation of mother is now finally abolished and given back ;
her person retreats. She is for the last time regarded as
mother, in order to be so no longer. This is involved in the
words "Behold they son!"—I am thy son no longer—as also
in the profound and significant crisis of farewell. The earthly
relation, which at Cana might not intrude into His office, is
now entirely dissolved. The dying Son of God and Saviour
of the world, afterwards exalted, has no longer a mother according to the flesh. Mary is not even mentioned in connection with the resurrection, and there is no account of any
special appearance of the Lord for her sake. In Acts 1 : 14
she appears for the last time as belonging to the little com-
pany of the disciples and to the Church.

" Behold thy mother," John 19 : 27. Does the Lord intend

to say to John, "She will take the place of a mother to thee"? Does He not rather say, "Thou shalt take My place and care for her"? John was to be the stay of Mary, and not Mary the stay of John. Mary was not to be to the disciple the representative of Jesus, but the disciple was to be to Mary the representative of Jesus. The dependence and need of help was not on the side of John but on that of Mary.   *   *

The Lord establishes, founds, and blesses here "the spiritual family life of His new kingdom." This new relationship in the love of Christ goes far beyond all relationships after the flesh.   *   *   That Mary had other sons subsequently born (in favor of which much contested though simply historical truth we have often declared our opinion) does not so enter into the case here as to make this testament (the bequest of His mother to St. John) an argument against it.   *   *   The children of His mother, to whom our Lord had as yet been unknown and an alien (Ps 69 : 8), could not possibly, as spiritually alien, take His place or be to Mary what Jesus had been, even after their conversion ; but John was in spirit no alien. The whole objection rests too much on external care. This the Lord, of course, included, but connects it with that inmost spiritual relation of love which could alone satisfy the heart of Mary, and which she would find most abundantly in the fellowship of John's spirit.—[DR. STIER, *On the Words of the Lord Jesus.*

CPSIA information can be obtained
at www.ICGtesting.com
Printed in the USA
LVIC061546260620
659091LV00004B/16